D1528894

LAMBORGHINI
AVENTADOR

BY CALVIN CRUZ

BELLWETHER MEDIA • MINNEAPOLIS, MN

TM

Are you ready to take it to the extreme?
Torque books thrust you into the action-packed world
of sports, vehicles, mystery, and adventure. These books
may include dirt, smoke, fire, and dangerous stunts.
WARNING: read at your own risk.

This edition first published in 2016 by Bellwether Media, Inc.

No part of this publication may be reproduced in whole or in part without written permission of the publisher.
For information regarding permission, write to Bellwether Media, Inc., Attention: Permissions Department,
5357 Penn Avenue South, Minneapolis, MN 55419.

Library of Congress Cataloging-in-Publication Data

Cruz, Calvin, author.
  Lamborghini Aventador / by Calvin Cruz.
    pages cm -- (Torque. Car crazy)
  Summary: "Engaging images accompany information about the Lamborghini Aventador. The combination
of high-interest subject matter and light text is intended for students in grades 3 through 7"--Provided by
publisher.
  Includes bibliographical references and index.
  Audience: 7-12.
  Audience: Grades 3-7.
  ISBN 978-1-62617-283-8 (hardcover : alk. paper)
  1. Lamborghini automobile--Juvenile literature. I. Title.
  TL215.L33C78 2016
  629.222'2--dc23
                                    2015009714

Printed in the United States of America, North Mankato, MN.

TABLE OF CONTENTS

A SPECTACULAR SHOW

The waiting crowd buzzes with excitement. Lamborghini is set to show off its new **supercar**. Many people have traveled from far away to see the new **model**. The car will appear any second.

Cameras are ready for the moment. The music grows louder, and the Aventador is finally driven out before the audience. The car brings cheers from the crowd.

Soon, people are able to see the car up close. The crowd admires the **V12 engine** in the rear of the car. The doors are opened to show the comfortable, sporty **interior**. The fans are impressed by the Aventador's power, performance, and **luxury**.

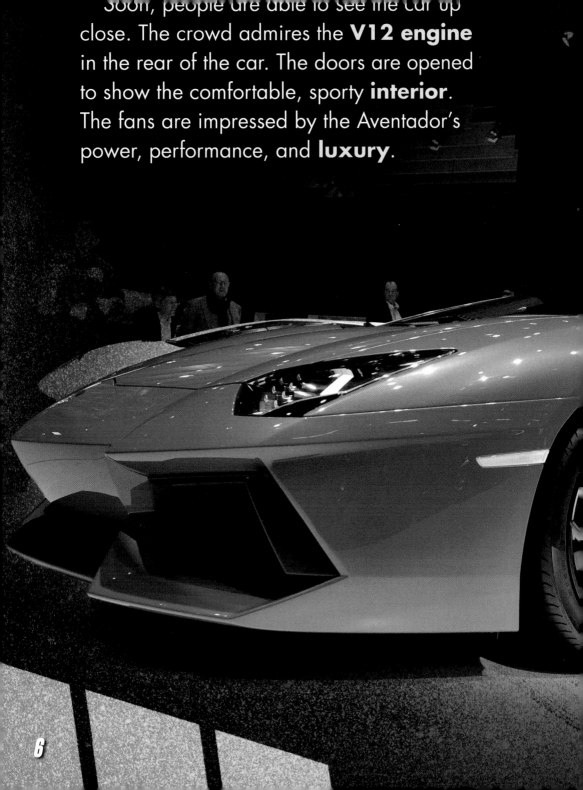

A BULLISH NAME
THE NAME *AVENTADOR* COMES FROM A PARTICULARLY BRAVE BULL THAT FOUGHT IN A BULLFIGHT IN SPAIN IN 1993.

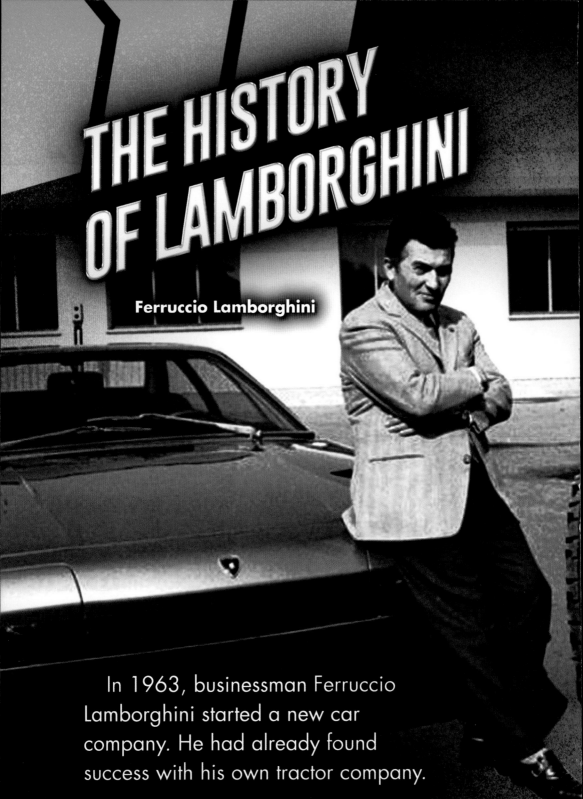

THE HISTORY OF LAMBORGHINI

Ferruccio Lamborghini

In 1963, businessman Ferruccio Lamborghini started a new car company. He had already found success with his own tractor company.

Now he wanted to make cars to compete with Ferrari and other sports car makers. Throughout the 1960s, Lamborghini Automobili was very successful.

Lamborghini tractor

1968 Lamborghini Miura

Sales slowed in the 1970s. Ferruccio was also losing control over his cars' designs. In 1973, he sold his company. Over the next 25 years, the Lamborghini name was bought and sold many times. The company often struggled.

Lamborghini Countach

2015 Lamborghini Huracán LP 610-4

In 1998, Lamborghini was purchased by Audi. It has since made many new and popular models. Lamborghini is back on track!

LAMBORGHINI AVENTADOR

The Aventador was first shown off at the 2011 Geneva Motor Show. It replaced Lamborghini's older Murciélago supercar.

The Aventador keeps many of the typical Lamborghini features. But the Aventador was made to perform better than any other car on the market. It can be purchased as either a **coupe** or a **roadster**.

EVEN MORE POWER

IN 2015, LAMBORGHINI SHOWED OFF THE AVENTADOR LP 750-4 SUPERVELOCE. THIS CAR HAS 750 HORSEPOWER AND A TOP SPEED OF MORE THAN 217 MILES (350 KILOMETERS) PER HOUR!

2012 Lamborghini Aventador LP 700-4 Coupe

TECHNOLOGY AND GEAR

The Aventador sits low to the ground. It is designed to be **aerodynamic**. Its body shape improves **acceleration**, allows turns at high speeds, and helps the car use less gas. **Carbon fiber** and **aluminum** parts are found throughout the body and interior. They keep the Aventador's weight low. This helps the V12 engine reach higher speeds.

2013 Lamborghini Aventador
LP 700-4 Roadster

V12 engine

The Aventador's engine is located in the rear of the car. It lies under a glass engine cover. Drivers have a lot of control over the look and feel of their Aventador. They choose the colors of the car's paint, carpets, leather, and stitching.

A driver can switch between three different drive settings. Each one changes the car's power and when it shifts gears. These settings also control the car's **wing**. The wing helps the Aventador grip the road in any driving condition. Drivers can also shift on their own using **paddle shifters** on the steering wheel.

wing

2015 LAMBORGHINI AVENTADOR LP 700-4 SPECIFICATIONS

CAR STYLE	COUPE OR ROADSTER
ENGINE	6.5L V12
TOP SPEED	217 MILES (350 KILOMETERS) PER HOUR
0 - 60 TIME	ABOUT 2.8 SECONDS
HORSEPOWER	691 HP (515 KILOWATTS) @ 8250 RPM
DRY WEIGHT	3,472 POUNDS (1,575 KILOGRAMS)
WIDTH	89.17 INCHES (226 CENTIMETERS)
LENGTH	188.19 INCHES (478 CENTIMETERS)
HEIGHT	44.72 INCHES (114 CENTIMETERS)
WHEEL SIZE	19 INCHES (48 CENTIMETERS) FRONT
	20 INCHES (51 CENTIMETERS) BACK
COST	STARTS AT $397,500

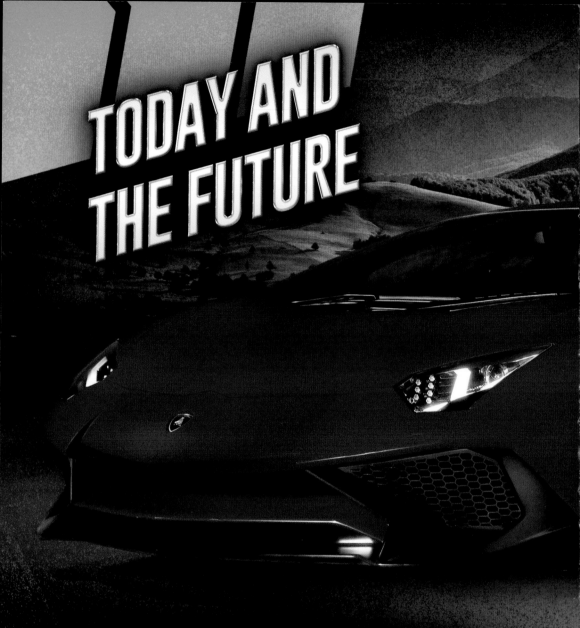

TODAY AND THE FUTURE

The Lamborghini Aventador continues to be a powerful, popular supercar. Drivers like the excitement of its smooth, fast ride. It has won many awards since it came out. Speed and adventure await behind the wheel of the Aventador!

BEST OF THE BEST
IN 2011, THE AVENTADOR WAS NAMED THE BEST SUPERCAR AT THE MIDDLE EAST MOTOR AWARDS. IT WAS ALSO NAMED *TOP GEAR'S* SUPERCAR OF THE YEAR.

HOW TO SPOT A LAMBORGHINI AVENTADOR

SHARP BODY LINES

REAR WING

SCISSOR DOORS

GLOSSARY

acceleration—an increase in speed

aerodynamic—having a shape that can move through air quickly

aluminum—a strong, lightweight metal

carbon fiber—a strong, lightweight material made from woven pieces of carbon

coupe—a car with a hard roof and two doors

interior—the inside of a car

luxury—expensive and offering great comfort

model—a specific kind of car

paddle shifters—paddles on the steering wheel of a car that allow a driver to change gears

roadster—a car with an open top and two seats

supercar—an expensive and high-performing sports car

V12 engine—an engine with 12 cylinders arranged in the shape of a "V"

wing—a part on the back of a car that helps the car grip the road

TO LEARN MORE

AT THE LIBRARY

Bow, James. *Lamborghini*. New York, N.Y.: Crabtree Pub., 2011.

Power, Bob. *Lamborghinis*. New York, N.Y.: Gareth Stevens Pub. Co., 2012.

Quinlan, Julia J. *Lamborghini*. New York, N.Y.: PowerKids Press, 2013.

ON THE WEB

Learning more about the Lamborghini Aventador is as easy as 1, 2, 3.

1. Go to www.factsurfer.com.

2. Enter "Lamborghini Aventador" into the search box.

3. Click the "Surf" button and you will see a list of related web sites.

With factsurfer.com, finding more information is just a click away.

INDEX